Analogue/Digital

Acknowledgements
Thanks to the editors of the following, in which some of these poems first appeared:

Axon: Creative Explorations, BBC Radio 3, *Illuminations, Iron, London Magazine, New Statesman & Society, The Spectator*

Asterisk (smith|doorstop 2011)
Bern Manifesto on climate change and cities (British Council 2005)
The Faber Book of Movie Verse (Faber 1992)
Feeling the Pressure (British Council 2008)
The Gregory Anthology 1987–1990 (Hutchinson 1990)
Northern Poetry II (Littlewood Arc 1991)
The Poetry Book Society Anthology 1989-1990 (Hutchinson 1989)
Poetry Introduction 7 (Faber 1990)
Quintet (Staple First Editions 1993)

'The Black Page' was one of 73 commissioned interpretations of the black page in *Tristram Shandy* by Laurence Sterne. It was included in an exhibition at Shandy Hall to celebrate the 250th anniversary of Volumes I & II of the book, page 73 of Volume I being a black page that marks the death of Parson Yorick. Sold by auction, the work is now in a private collection. http://www.blackpage73.blogspot.com

Analogue/Digital

New & Selected Poems

Paul Munden

smith|doorstop

Published 2015 by
smith|doorstop Books
The Poetry Business
Bank Street Arts
32-40 Bank Street
Sheffield S1 2DS
www.poetrybusiness.co.uk

ISBN 978-1-910367-37-7

British Library Cataloguing-in-Publication Data.
A catalogue record for this book is available from the
British Library.

Typeset by Utter
Printed by Printondemand.com
Cover image: David Platts, The Wood, 1979-80,
pastel & chalk on canvas
Author photo: Chris Tribble

smith|doorstop is a member of Inpress,
www.inpressbooks.co.uk. Distributed by Central Books Ltd.,
99 Wallis Road, London E9 5LN.

The Poetry Business is an Arts Council
National Portfolio Organisation

Supported by
**ARTS COUNCIL
ENGLAND**

Contents

New Poems, 2013–14

Poems, 1986–2011

One to a Hundred

The Pale Rider and his gang drift off
into the woods and I'm left alone,
flat on my back, staring up
through the trees – my right hand
still holding the Colt 45.

The high-noon sun's so strong
I go for the eyes-shut approach
but should I keep my body stiff
or relax? I fear my heart-beat
will give me away.

The silence stretches out.
I'm beginning to lose count
and rather enjoy it when
a different sense of unease
creeps over me.

What if they've left me for good?
What if they're changing the rules
or inventing a whole new game?

Kiss Chase

Boy plus girl was just an idea.
I chased the same one time
after time – trust me to pick
the fastest of her sex.

Lessons I don't remember
but reading, writing
must have rubbed off
amongst all the fun.

Now my playground legs
are made of lead,
so many faces darting away
before I wake and you're *it*.

Hell Creek

The dinosaurs came this way. They knew
this small town Saturday sunshine
lazing into the store for beers
until their muscles seized, braincells seized.

Why did we fall for the cute buffalo
in our rucksacks, each with a girl
back home in mind? We dashed off
postcards – *see you no doubt before*

this arrives – as we played with a route:
Clear Lake, Badlands, Rapid City ...
our glasses, idle, beaded with sweat,
spanning the ragged patchwork of the USA.

We were sitting on a grassy verge,
back from the road, under trees, when
a cartoon dust-clap stammered to a halt
and a burned out Angel greeted us

like long lost friends. We were zombies
hovering in his mirrored shades.
Beneath his rancid sleeveless denim
a bare torso was snaked with tattoos.

Haven't you heard? Where've you guys been!
I've chucked it all and bought this jeep.
Alaska is the place to go. Wanna ride?
The snow ahead looked close enough to lick

but the jeep was a wreck, his luggage
a single spade. We'd no faith
in his battered speech taking
him, let alone us, beyond the next bend.

Test Flight
(Ham, 31/6/61)

I guessed it was a tree-house of the future.
We used to play in it, we used to be buddies.
Then they strapped me in and said goodbye.

I got over the sickness and braved the view:
the breathtaking blue, the browns and greens
of a map I'm not supposed to have seen.

Doubles

1 *(After Evelyn Waugh)*

Embedded diamonds spell her name.
A living casket – it skids
on the polish and is put back to GO.

'What will you do when it is dead?'
asked Mr Samgrass. 'Can you have
another tortoise fitted to the shell?'

Don't laugh: these things happen.
But I wonder if my pain, grafted
to another's, will shrivel or swell?

2 *(After T H White)*

The story has it that all ships
go more slowly when carrying
the right foot of a tortoise on board.

So when the wind dropped
and the lumbering stowaway was found
below deck, your course was clear.

But you were worried, not knowing
your right from your left,
so you chopped off the other two too.

Chameleon

Your emotions are a give-away –
green with envy, black with rage.

Your wandering eyes look loopy
but they're speed-reading the world

and for more than the gist.
One is fixed on a beetle for lunch

while the other patrols the borders
for thieving geckos and skinks.

You're prepared for the worst:
if a colour-zone changes on the map

then a nifty swop of battledress
steadies your goggling pulse.

Misericords

The pelican, feeding
her murdered fledglings
with blood from her own breast
is a symbol of redemption.

A musician is often a pig
blowing his own trumpet,
a cat on the fiddle
or a stray dog, trained

to maul a badger's guts.
The doctor
is a curious monkey
perusing a urine flask.

There's a preference
for mythical beasts –
griffins, gorgons
and the popular phoenix –

though one carpenter
had clearly seen
the elephant
presented to Henry III.

Mermaids represent
the lure of the flesh.
Souls are fish,
innocently gawping.

Virgins are useful
for capturing unicorns,
while spinsters must guide
bachelor apes through hell.

As for the housewife,
she bludgeons her husband
with a faggot. It's true
he's a buffoon,

a dim Green Man;
his gormless face framed
in a wicker contraption
masked with leaves.

It's all good sport.
There's hare-hunting,
bear-baiting, football
and St George

in full armour
riling the dragon
who has a thick neck
for each of seven sins.

The shepherd retrieves
his sheep, the dove
bears an olive branch
and Jonah appears

to have made friends
with the whale.
Only the Baptist's head on a plate
looks steadfastly glum.

It's a feast for the eyes –
so much that I crave
a quick reprieve,
some simpler treat.

Crocodile

I still can't make head or tail
    of the shape you claim to see

in the slime-covered pantiles
    from your bedroom window

though I myself was once part
    of a chain of green caps slinking

across the cathedral close at dusk
    without a thought for the literal world.

The Winchester Diver

For five years, daily, he seals himself
into a monastic, rubberized suit
with only his two pink frond-like hands
protruding. His feet are lead weights.
His bulbous, brass-cased head
is pure Science Fiction. The Lagoon Man.
He spits on the eye-piece to prevent it misting,
more out of habit than to any effect.
Within a minute he's working blind,
his own slow progress stirring
further sediment in the lugubrious drift
right under the foundations. The sound
of the cathedral choir wafts down
but there's no hint of what permeates
his brain throughout the numbing routine.
His sledgehammer sledgehammers on. Blocks
of water-logged peat are packed into bucket
after bucket until at last his fingers rasp
against shingle, a good moment to surface
for a smoke – nicotine to protect him
from the diseased, graveyard swamp
in which he works.

Is that a tease, like the walrus moustache?
Looking at the photographs is going
back with him, shoring up each trench
with a similar commitment.
Down come sacks of cement to lug
into place. Calmly, he slits every throat
and pumps pressurized grout into the cracks
between each slumped and saturating corpse.
The shifting ground becomes a monolith
fit to take the strain of a millennium.

As he starts to tire, he jerks the lifeline
and lets a shot of air billow
around his midriff, forcing him up again
into the rush of light.

The Apprentice

He was digging himself into a hole
approximately the size of himself
and assuming it was virgin soil.
No one had told him otherwise.
No one had told him anything
but to dig. How then was he to know
the headstone had been removed
for an additional inscription until,
with a muffled crunch, his feet
were in the coffin and his heart
was in his mouth.

The Practice Room

His voice was a stony bass, rinsed
with meths. One side of his cassock
sagged with the tell-tale bottle
and when he leaned across to turn
the page, there was the smell.

In the dingy room, his fingers
were yellow ivory, exacting hammers
that taught me Hindemith. My progress
was painful, and still is. I explained
about dividing my time with the violin

at which he took my hands
and felt the flexible knuckles ripple
in his grasp. I try it myself now
and it just won't work.

✳

The room turned into a Victorian parlour.
She came and went like a ghost,
her grey hair a frizzed silhouette
against the window, beyond which
other boys played cricket in the yard.

She believed in letting the bow ride free.
Before, you had to hold – later imagine –
a book under the arm. All this
she said in a whispering vibrato
that seemed to brush my skin.

It's been a long time. My violin slides out
from a silk scarf. We uncork the wine.
The piano gives an A for me to crank
the stiff pegs up to the mark.

Home Movies

A slice of oak announces where we lived
and the disconnected, wobbly moments
when a camera was at hand.
                          A car
is always pulling up and guests pile out.
Thinking about it, they must have
reversed then driven in once more
when we were ready to film.
I'm dressed as Robin Hood – and, OK,
still happy with a feather in my cap
but I wouldn't be seen dead
in those green tights.
The bow-string slackens
after every shot. I run forward
to pick up my arrow which falls just short
of the target and again, run forward
to pick up the arrow which falls just short.
The target is chipboard on which
Dad has painted bright concentric circles
focusing on the scarlet gold.

                      ✳

It's all there, wound up in my head.
Composition: 'Holidays'. Now it clicks
through the projector's gate.

> *This Easter I packed up*
> *our family house,*
> *sorting the years*
> *of garage junk,*
> *hauling whole suitcases*
> *down to the bonfire.*
> *Dad didn't move*

from his bed.
Mum was with him
except when his pain
got to her nerves.
The vicar was called.
We gathered round
while he said a prayer
and I went rigid
as Dad's eyes opened
in panic, believing
this was it. He hung on
for days after that.
I was holding his hand
when suddenly I knew
he wasn't there.

✳

I'm on my bike, concentrating hard
on the curve around the lawn.
I swerve, with the briefest of smiles,
and here's Dad, waiting to step in
to deal with my gravel-rashed knees.
The reel's used up on a weekend visitor
backing her car down the drive.
White dots perforate the last few frames.
Then there's the slap of film spinning
freely on the take-up spool.

Gutting the ABC

After years of corporate mismanagement
it's over, box-office slumping to a few
Maltesers melting from hand to mouth.

The whole facade is down. I stand
where the screen used to be, adding
a soundtrack to events as I see them –
the earth movers ripping out seats.

My backside would numb just waiting
for the feature: globs of swirling colour
were accompanied by Easy Listening Hits.
Then Pearl and Dean.
                              Is memory doomed
to be demolished when I'm old, hard
of hearing and with failing sight,
or will a colossal bottle of Gordon's
still pour its juniper cascade
and a voice-over sell me a carpet
whose gash pattern you wouldn't believe?

Honeymoon

We were the last of our species inhabiting
the vast beach. The sun still shone
out of season, if too weakly for most.
The tinny Suzuki revved and scuffed
through sand – hair in the wind, we were
sure of a soft fall.
        You'd reached the end
of the only book you had. We tried
sharing my page but I was far too slow
so we tore *The French Lieutenant's Woman*
in half.
        You began while I finished
and for once, reading didn't seem
the usual rift.
        The sun thinned.
We returned to the hotel and pushed
the narrow twin beds back together.

A New Arrival

When I imagined the Big Time it was not
in the basement of Broadcasting House
stepping up between Peter Porter
and Anthony Thwaite to the white urinal.

*

Paul Munden, Paul Muldoon. Hugh, you
introduced us over a glass of wine,
your mulled voice muddling the occasion.
I was a wisp, while the maestro was –
dare I say it – well-heeled, plump
as a prize mushroom. He leaned forward
to catch my name again, stumbling
on another of his magical half-rhymes.

*

The promotion was half-baked.
It was a double bill and Selima's photo
read Adams not Hill.

I was putting her up for the night.
It was late, and when we got back
you'd gone to bed. You'd also gone to town

on our country kitchen, with french bread,
cheese, and a hand-made plate of fruit
like a stiff napkin, topped with strawberries.

Strange for the two of you to meet first
over breakfast. In just a few more weeks
we'd have a regular, little-known guest.

Skiffle

The bass is a long piece of elastic
stretched on a broomstick.
An empty barrel of homebrew
doubles as a drum

and this is just the formal set.
You're free to join in
with an improvised maraca –
that handy jar of rice.

My baby daughter beats
not-quite-time with a wooden spoon
on a saucepan: I click a pen
against my teeth.

Sometimes, as now, words
are all there is; sometimes
the sound carries no further
than this room.

The Little Nipper

Happy Chris Mouse. Marketing's gift
for turning the seasonal language
into slush was luckily lost on you.
Your fingers scrabbled at the eyes,
the cherry nose, fluffing the rosy cheeks.
We moved the dining-table out

and brought in an old settee from the barn
to make a comfortable playroom.
What worried us was worm
but the next day's evidence –
tissue paper pinked into a ragged doily –
suggested our pests were furry friends.

The local hardware store supplied me
with 'The Little Nipper'. I cut a square
of cheese and lodged it on the spike,
the steel spring snapping forward
several times before it was triggered.
I dreamed that sound all night.

And in the morning, there he was,
jaw squashed by the steel,
eyes still locked in a black stare.
I put you safely behind bars
with your monster-sized cuddly toy.
'Play with that while I deal with this.'

I lifted the trap complete with victim
dangling by the nose but the tail
brushed the back of my hand
and a shiver scooted up my arm and around
my shoulders. You liked the glow
in the coals as I tossed it on the range.

That's What This Is

You lunge, lock on to the teat of your bottle
like a little prop forward into the scrum,

and you look the part in your stripes,
with mauled ears, chubby cheeks, thin on hair.

You found your feet – there they were
all the time! How long before I'm telling you

to pull up your socks? Already the struggle is on
for independence, with breakfast the battleground.

I offer a finger of toast but you want the piece
on my plate. I let you taste it in order to believe

it's one and the same thing. You catch sight
of yourself in the mirror: an identical baby

smiles out. It's all so hard to grasp.
Toys do help, with chunky controls, mechanics

that a microchip could handle in its sleep.
Push that lever and Humpty Dumpty's head slices

off into your lap. Pull this, and you bring
my own forgotten childhood back to life.

Shared memory is as much of a bond as the bond
of the flesh. My father's gone

but his friend of some seventy years tells me
how they once shared a desk. It could be yesterday.

Mind Your Head

And now it's happened a thousand times
you still don't see it. A message
goes to the brain but loses itself
in some sudden distraction –
a phone call, or whistling kettle ...
You still don't see.

My mother finally dropped
to the kitchen floor
without such casual mishap,
colliding instead with something stronger
though invisible: the irresistible dark
starburst in her head.

October 31st

Surely we saw it coming –
our anniversary, doomed
to double as Halloween?

The children stood by
as you scooped the mush of pips
from a pumpkin, saving it

for some ghoulish pie.
Lara was hooked as your knife
plunged into the blank expanse of skin

to form the triangular holes
we called eyes. It was she
who devised the two faces:

a friendly smile for ourselves
and a terrifying stare to fend off
those restless spirits of the night.

It grew dark. We lit a candle
in the bowl of the head
then watched her bright idea

backfire – the scary visage
reflecting in the window, mocking
our happiness from outside.

Freeze-Frame

Plonked in front of the TV
already she's jabbing h-
      ERR!
-emote control in search
of cartoon action or the god-
      DAM!
ads. Scary how still she is
though her mind is leapin-
      GAH!
-ead. She's a little editor
at large but the TV's ca-
      UGH!
-t on. Dramas no longer pause
for fear of the audience swi-
      TCH!
-ing allegiance. There'll be
time for reflection, the
      BOO!
-k of the series, complete
with inserts on ho-
      WAP!
-rogramme is made, for those
of us who dream of the
      POW!
-er to create what we see.
Mum dozes. She's lost the n-
      ARR!
-ative but her daughter
insists there's a really
      GOO!
-d bit at the end, meaning
where the body lands on a sp-
      IKE!

The Generation Game

Take a careful look at what is passing
before your eyes:

    the nest of teak tables
    the cut-glass decanter
    the snakeskin bag
    the snake
    the tropical forest
    the chalice of spawn
    the prime beach, ripe for development
    the loggerhead turtle
    the hobby-horse
    the ark
    the trappings of authority
    the bribe to enlist
    the anonymous blood
    the feud
    the poisoned pen
    the withdrawal of funds
    the hungry child
    the memorial silence
    the excuse

You've thirty seconds, starting from now:
whatever you remember can be yours.

Möschberg

I walk from the hothouse of debate
into the icy hillside wind which strips
all thought back to the bone.

I scan the horizon for a view
of the mountains, but it's all cloud,
and darkening. In the valley,

one by one, tiny lights prick out
a new map of the village and beyond,
the grey skies suddenly pulling

apart – and the Jungfrau,
like a beacon, summoning me
to a once-more-possible task.

Back inside, the mood has mellowed
to a warm camaraderie. We re-group
at tables lined with bottled water

in rows, the economists, scientists
and engineers all with graph-paper pads
while I wrestle with this unruly page.

Half Truths

50% of accidents are avoidable;
50% of plans are ill-conceived.

50% of cities are in rural areas;
50% of people sleep under the stars.

50% of facts are accurate;
50% of deceit lacks charm.

50% of politicians misuse statistics;
50% are misunderstood.

50% of all energy is wasted;
50% of waste is a case in point.

50% is an average mark-up;
50% of mediocrity is worse than crass.

50% of depression is clinical;
50% of madness is inspired.

50% of failures are unsubstantiated;
50% of progress is just marking time.

50% of hopes are legally binding;
50% of fears are not scary enough.

50% of science is invaluable;
50% of poems are unread.

50% of everything is a generalization;
50% of nothing is less than you think.

The Riverside Arms

The landlord pulls a pint
and the foam surges
over the rim of the glass.

On the wall is a chart
of previous floods,
a living graph of how

Matt, in '31, stood with water
lapping at the heels
of his Wellington boots;

Cameron, in '45, sat
with his G&T waist deep
at this warping table;

Susan, in '68, had to hold
her glass of white head high
to keep it dry;

and Michelle, in '82, finally
let that shot of drambuie
slip from her grasp

into the rising tide
like a depth charge
and felt her earrings

tugged upwards
like buoys
or fisherman's floats ...

In the following century
it's a different tale:
the barman dispenses

neat measures of scotch
and vodka from the optics
while the electric pump

drizzles beer to a thin line
that shows precisely where
enough is enough.

Obsession

Every night, an alphabet of girls' names
rattles the roof tiles, one storm
after another, howling through your head.

One in particular won't subside, haunts you
with a glimpse of earrings in the crowd
or a whiff of perfume, catching your breath.

You renovate a space in your heart,
then your home, but only her absence
comes to stay, and no one (but no one) sleeps.

Agnes 1972
Alicia 1983
Allison 2001
Anita 1977
Audrey 1957
Betsy 1965
Beulah 1967
Camille 1969
Carla 1961
Carmen 1974
Carol 1954
Celia 1970
Cleo 1964
Connie 1955
Diana 1990
Diane 1955
Donna 1960
Dora 1964
Edna 1968
Elena 1985
Eloise 1975
Fifi 1974
Flora 1963

Fran 1996
Frances 2004
Gloria 1985
Hattie 1961
Hazel 1954
Hilda 1964
Hortense 1996
Inez 1966
Ione 1955
Iris 2001
Isabel 2003
Isidore 2002
Janet 1955
Joan 1988
Katrina 2005
Lili 2002
Marilyn 1995
Michelle 2001
Opal 1995
Paloma 2008
Rita 2005
Roxanne 1995
Wilma 2005

New Poems, 2013–14

Risk Assessment

Julius Caesar, Northallerton Leisure Centre, 2004

A sudden drum-beat hits you
and the house lights fail.
It's not a good start.

Out of the gloom,
flickering neon electrics
crack and sizzle

as if frazzling flies
on their dodgy voltage,
simulating a prophetic storm.

It's only a matter of time
before the knives are out
and blood is let centre stage

in a bucket. I can feel it
greasing my own forearms
like those of an accomplice.

Then come the insinuations,
sharper weapons still, flung
into every corner of the theatre.

The interval offers a reprieve
– the known world
of *do not take drinks*

back into the auditorium –
but it's a token gesture;
the real damage has been done.

We wince, as Cinna –
who could be any one of us –
is strung up on the scaffold

and when the automatic rifles
are brandished on all sides,
there's nowhere to hide.

Observing Silence

Twenty-two black armbands form
a mute circle in the centre of the pitch.
A single amplified voice calls for silence
and the crowd complies. What follows

is harder to detect: the soundless echo
of a car crash in a tunnel, a rippling
bafflement, like the tremors we have felt
beneath our own two feet which then shake

loose the stone blocks of a cathedral,
its cracked spire falling as heavy dust.
Every fragment of personal loss
adds its tiny complicating weight.

There's no dissent, no drunk to beat
the whistle. It's a sonic vacuum so intense
the technology shuts down. No signal
...

...
but then the first little hand-clap
sets off the static of massive applause
and the airwaves crackle back to life.

Occasional Noise

I listen hard
to nothing more than a twig
breaking underfoot,

the sweet, sweet
arrivals of tiny birds
in the lemon trees

and a lizard
rustling across gravel
into the leaves.

The invisible cicadas
don't even compete
with the singing

of my own ears
or the rhythm section
leaking from an iPod.

A fat fly, mindlessly
curious, cruises
past my nose,

a pigeon flaps
its tea-towel wings
from roof to roof

and a distant dog barks,
waking its own impatience
and repeating itself.

From way downhill
comes a faint, Italian rant
into a mobile phone

while further up,
with the bronzed clarity
of afternoon sun,

a cowbell monitors
the homeward plod
of a solitary cow.

There's a skittering
of wind, and the sound
I imagine a butterfly

might make disappearing
into the night.
Across the valley,

the tell-tale taps
of a hammer are building
an identical quiet.

The Last TV Detector Van

is in your area. A predatory insect in fancy dress,
crawling the kerb,

        it has hours to kill,

armed with mumbo jumbo
about oscillations, frequencies ...
a prog rocker twiddling the dials of a Moog,
it's becoming a bit of a joke.

It's beginning to look like a busman's holiday.
It's beginning to look conspicuously out of date,
drawing attention to itself
in all the wrong ways, its old-hat camouflage
inside out.

        Or is that the point?

Parked for too long, it's a conspiracy theory.
Either that, or the driver has fallen asleep,
while a rebel surveillance gets underway
behind twitching net curtains.

As it drives into the distance,
the signal begins to fade. Soon it will be no more
than a fabled beast with fabled powers,
finally rumbled.

        It haunts me.

Dream Mile

My creaking knees
are an anachronism,
metres coming up
against yards

as another old-timer
puts his creased thumb
to the wheel and calls us
to our marks.

Analogue

My daughter's heartbeat
peaks as a beam of light
onscreen, transcribed

by a jiggling pen –

my father's hand shaking
like a teleprinter ready
for the final scores.

Digital

The sat-nav takes us
to the cemetery gate, beyond which
I'm hard-wired to identify

the headstone: the deleted

dates and names my daughter
retrieves, cleaning them
with her bare fingers.

Forensics

1

The leather case has seen better days
– and worse, judging by these gouges,
clearly from a two-handed grip
of some desperation. The straps
have been subjected to abnormal stress,
bearing the weight of something more
than just the case and its contents.
As for the violin, the original varnish
has been compromised, most probably
by lengthy immersion. Chemical tests
suggest sea water, authentic.
The bridge is completely missing
and only two, slack strings – the A and D –
remain, certainly of no further musical use.

2

Gold fountain pen, "W. H. H." ;
diamond solitaire ring ;
silver cigarette case ;
letters ;
silver match box, "To W.H.H., from Collingson's staff, Leeds" ;
telegram to Hotley, Bandmaster "Titanic" ;
nickel watch ;
gold chain ;
gold cigar holder ;
stud ;
scissors ;
16 s ;
16 cents ;
coins.

3

At some stage the little life-raft
slips from your grasp and the story
is adrift. The straps float free
like strands of thick dark kelp,
swaying to a lullaby
that still sings in your fingers
as your waterlogged boots
and heavy brown overcoat
– pockets full of silver and gold –
drag you down.
Your stiff upper lip now
is all about ice; your violin
in its sodden cradle
the survivor, already buoyant with myth.

Scrimshaw

A skeletal sperm whale hangs
as if carved from the air;
on the walls, blackened harpoons
and all the grim ironmongery
by which once blubbery grace
was dismantled. I watch
the slow inklings
of pity and terror flicker
across your face, though were you
not my own flesh and blood
I couldn't read you. I want to reach
for your hand but you're too far away

and getting further. Every step
through the great hall is whittling
your innocence. I feel a tonnage
of sentiment slip and roll
beneath the knives, knives called *spades*,
with head-strap and throat-chain
in cahoots. The blankets are stripped
back and strung up like euphemisms
seen for what they are,
such a bulk of beauty processed
into utility and waste.
It's all too much. We escape

to the galleries of remedial art,
the simple whalebone tools, handles,
hinges and busks, leading to more
whimsical scrimshanderings engraved
with a rough needle or scraped
with patience into miniature marvels –
a fully rigged ship, replica of the vessel

56

on whose decks the brutal hours
were whiled away, whiting out
in a finickety craze: twin mirrors
reflecting obsession to infinity.
Ten years stand between us

and the devil detail. I confront
my own memory, scrawled
with cruel reminders
and rebukes that cut happiness
to the quick. Your hand
may be nearer now but mine
withdraws, fearful of recruiting you
to more difficult truth.
We bide our time,
slam together tumblers of rum,
rub soot into these scribbles
and oil them to a loving gleam.

New England

On the road into Vermont
the loggers' trucks are hauling logs
that look like half a forest

until you see the forest.

How much wood ...

Every so many miles
a small, repetitive shape half-
glimpsed from the car window

and already a hundred –
two hundred yards behind us
punctuates our journey.

No one mentions it and so
it becomes a weird embodiment
of silence, waddling on the verge,

flattening itself into the landscape

like something run over

or a tongue-twister
dawdling in the memory
when what you're trying to do is forget.

Maggot

Step onto the grass ...
You know this from a dream
or a book, maybe a painting –
Fra Angelico perhaps: daisies
with perfect little pleated white petals
centring on a honeycombed sun.
You know them in a fresco
of innocent ciphers, never before
as a living tapestry of stars at your feet.

You want to feel the cool petals
between your toes, walk barefoot
deeper into the scene, following
a daisy-chain of *love-me, love-me-*
... throwing away the *nots*.

The day grows hotter, the shadows
more intense. The stars darken
to blotches of purpled crimson.
You find one, then another,
with childlike excitement
until some dull instinct
(the spoilsport – or is that me?)
draws your gaze to a tree, arching
above the cloistered grass, cherries
and more cherries becoming visible
within the canopy of leaves.

You've seen cherries before
without ever conceiving of this tree
towering over you with such sweet plenty.
You want to taste, to eat ... you stoop
to pick a fallen cherry from the ground
and turn it in your fingers
testing its promise:

cherry,
                    cherry ...

I want you to find that perfect fruit
and it's not happening.
                    One branch
hangs within my reach,
and I imagine I could bend it
low enough for you to pluck a cherry
of your choice – but nothing gives.
You turn again to your eager search,
your fingers growing sticky
with a cherried gloss.

In the middle of the lawn
sits a plain wooden box-room
with a narrow staired entrance
and a sign:
                    Maggot.
                    Please no ...

Where can it lead if not out
of this sumptuous world
into some putrefying terror, or worse –
the crushing banal. Don't go ...

Don't step beyond the grass,
the daisies, the cherries,
the painting, the dream ...
In the book at least I know
that for as long as I watch over you,
you're here:
                    not gone, *not* gone, *not.*

Divertimenti

La Galleria d'Arte Moderna di Milano

In the courtyard, bronze women,
rooted to the spot, let their fingers
become twigs, reaching for the sky;
women working out how to be trees.
I love them.
                    A name on a poster
catches my eye: *Patrizia*. A tree?

Patrizia
          Patricia
                    Practica
                              Practice ...

In the garden, women line up
in a sequence of copper silhouettes,
some pregnant, some already
with babies, playfully catching the light.

I'm taking this in my stride, free
of any need to understand or worse –
explain. Inside, little bronze du animals
– an otter with a woman's breasts
and a swan woman – usher me

upstairs, where the rows of figures
are altogether more strange, clothed,
whispering to their neighbours.
There's still an hour until my train
so I join them, and hear a name:

Patrizia,
           not a tree after all,
                       a woman
sitting poised at the grand piano
at the end of the gallery, dark ringlets
framing her impossibly pretty face,
focused on the keys, and when her fingers
begin their caress I think fuck
the train, and I know I'm not alone.

The music is tender and thunderous
by turns. We're all transported,
but as her foot works the pedal,
something starts to nag. *Trainers?*

It's as if she's heard me, and glances
around, showing a faint irritation.
The end is in sight but she's lost it,
starts something else, and even this
she doesn't seem to want to complete.
And as I work through excuses
on her behalf, it dawns on me
that this is just *practice*, now closing
without her giving the final chord
its full weight, like the poet
who suddenly speeds up, or tails off,
or simply has his butterfly mind
on the next poem, which is called

Il Museo della Musica di Venezia

Where are you? Shopping? I stroll
into the cool of San Maurizio,
a haven from the crowds, listening
to the curious silence of violins:
some by Amati, some his pupils,
patient apprentices kept behind glass.
I pause by a viola d'amore, reading
how the lower strings resonate
when the top set are played.
The thin, piped Vivaldi doesn't do it.

But here are the true understudies,
their pale scalloped backs half-
finished in the deserted workroom
at the back of the church, glued
and clamped, awaiting the purfling
of fine poplar and pearwood
to enhance their almost erotic curves,
and the varnish to enrich their tone.

Except, I realize, these young violins
will never sound. It's all a stage,
the luthier's tools put aside
with too deliberate thought,
these poor albinos kept in the dark,
away from the Red Priest's touch
that would make them sing.
Never for them the embarrassment
of mistakes, or the secret, late-night
grappa-fuelled musical risks
they hear of, dumb with disbelief.

This and That

I'm clearing out the shed, as more of this
and that is still making its way in: hard drives
with no memory, clad in see-through plastic
curves that say *look I'm still pretty;*
so much cobwebbed state of the art.
An intercom is strung along the landing
to my parents, who don't answer. Boxed
with the footballers – wobbly little gods,
each astride their half of the globe –
cricketers in baggy green caps
are still waiting for an innings.
Relegated to this dim underworld,
do they – when I'm not watching –
come out to play? There's flesh-pink paint
with which to touch them up, flesh-pink all-sorts,
as if flesh is the colour to which everything
fades: here, an earpiece on a twin-coiled cable
like a medical appliance. Elvis on flesh-pink vinyl
turns on an ancient turntable, ruined
by needles and shaky hands. Spilling coils
of tape are no better, warbling with a vibrato
stretched in the deck of an old Capri.

It gets harder, dealing with things already
cleared out; things that were never here;
things for which I never made room –
a wireless, with irreplaceable valves,
still capable of the warm, walnut hum
of my mother's kitchen, wanting only
the airwaves from a different age;
things existing only in my head but still
cluttering this space: a painting by a lover
herself long gone when *that* made room
for *this*, this for that. Can't I have it all?

I'm lying here in the dark, shifting things
from those darker corners where darkness
warps into something darker still. Hung
on a rusty nail is a rust-coloured jerkin
that's seen it all – and more. I slip my arms
through the stiff leather, walk to the clearing
at the top of the woods where a bonfire
still smoulders. One by one, I crumple papers
and release them, watching how they
open again, bright flowers, before curling
in on themselves as flakes of black;
the documents of a life, all that –
and then this, sent up in smoke.

The Empty Room

After the reading, we fell
into the lobby bar, demob happy,
but when someone asked me the time
I was already in the elevator
– stomach plummeting –

back to the twenty-seventh floor
of the snowbound Baltimore hotel,
heading for the room where I had placed
my father's gold watch on the lectern
to keep me from losing track.

The Hospital Clock

Your breast cancer
has been removed.
We wait

for the necessary papers,
the temporary all-clear
allowing us to leave

the building, collect
the car and quit
the whole abominable limbo –

the pull,
      pull,
           pull

of the clock without enough
power to haul its hand
around the dial.

Rediffusion

The colour is a little drained
in the afternoon sun, but squint
and you'll just make out
the blue icing that I insisted
should represent the sea.
Model dinosaurs stretch their necks
into a forest of candles.
I can count eight
so that must have been my age.
My pet tortoise lumbers into view,
scrunching nasturtiums.

※

The backdrop changes
to a lawn thickly embroidered
with dandelions. I'm expecting
the familiar miracle
as I lift the stony body
from its straw-lined vault
but there's a darkening blot
of blood sealing each eye.
At the crazy-paved line
of the mouth a bubble of blood
is almost like hope, like childhood.

※

My daughter opens the roof
of a house I know
in every miniature detail
– except the occupants.
An aproned frog serves plastic ham

to her eager guests. A badger
drinks from a tiny pewter tankard
crested with a Whitbread stag.
A mouse sits at the grand piano,
remastering the soundtrack
to this my new life.

✳

Stepping stones (so small!)
take her back across the stream
with a man of her own
to picnics where we would listen
for the steam train passing
from some black and white film
– *grey, as* she called it,
waving to strangers who lean out
now with their camera-phones,
our gestures relayed
ever further into the unknown.

Harbour Swim

And here they come, every one a winner,
    glimpses
of my father's face, beaming
under a skull cap, his thick arms
greased with lard, slogging
against the tide, current,

                        undertow, the *rip*
                of waters fifty years warmer,
           where a girl's graceful crawl
                  – no, *freestyle* –
      is shadowed by sharks, the snap
       of his trophy her lucky charm.

Dead Reckoning

Slowly, meticulously, you replace
the new brass quadrant
in its mahogany case; the lead-
weighted line, magnetic compass
and mariner's astrolabe all idle
as you ponder the unknown horizon,
the unsettling swell. Your thoughts
are strangely becalmed.
You need to go back, way back

                    to what else you know, realign
                 your senses, gauge the depth of water
             by its colour, feel the changing weather
              through the movement of birds,
                     taste the danger in the air.
              When you finally make it out,
                 some will call it *guesswork*
                 at which you'll smile and agree,
                    having nothing to lose.

A New and Correct Map of the World

#1

The little clay tablet is cracked
across the dial where a river
leads south from mountain
to swamp.
        And that's it –
the four corners of the earth
cradled in your palm
like an all-purpose gadget.

#2

Where knowledge runs out,
the artist, all at sea, conjures
a monstrous fish from the folds
of vellum, so expressively drawn
it surely has something urgent
to tell you, some intimation
of how everything will change,
but it's too far-fetched,
too terrible, too soon.

#3

Someone has remembered
the winds (two with turbans)
and the stars, overlaid like a net
to catch our dreams.

Paradise, which I think of
as a bar in the Giardini,
is a world apart, a fortress
to the right of the parchment crease.

#4

The eastern coast of *Nouvelle Hollande*
requires a theory (French, of course)
but oh dear, what a lifeless attempt,
such a crude apology
for a cartographer's line
made ragged by the surf.

#5

Grains of red sand shift in the breeze
and the software is updated.

The National Library is re-named
for the day as Shell Australia

and the scholars lose their bearings,
gawping at ancient shipments

of kerosene, and a liquefied gas plant
floating in the north-west.

The red sand is crushed house-brick.
Walk on it and listen to marching troops.

#6

You wake today bereft and look
for solace as always in the sea.
You know these waters
like the back of your hand, shaped
to cut a familiar pathway
through the waves, but this morning,
surging out of the beautiful blue
      comes the whale
in all its corporeal grandeur,
its gentle fatherly bulk
befriending you, skin to skin.

Bless the fellow traveller, who
treading water, levels her hi-tech lens
to your new world: fixed, and true.

Summer

The heat intensifies. Tarmac
   cracks and glistens.
The bush combusts,
               birds
fall from the sky.

Someone will remember
the exact time and date when Summer
was suddenly too soft a word.

People stare blankly
at the niceties of centigrade.
Scientists calculate predictive
curves.
      It's the weathermen
in their outlandish ties
who know best – that what we need

is a new colour.

Outback

I waited patiently for provisions
to be packed. I needed nothing
except, perhaps, animal tracks
in the soles of my shoes
and a compass in one heel

but whether we drove the first
of the mere two miles to the sea
or walked all the way, I lived
for the moment I would escape
at the half-hidden turning

into the woods, where I followed
my self-made path of tree-roots
lining the compacted peat
like giant marbled veins, polished
by the rub of my feet – leaping

from one familiar point of balance
to the next, through the deep
shade of tall story-book pines
and rhododendrons, in a rush
of excitement I didn't want to end.

Once, I thought I saw a snake,
the zigzag of an adder
twisting beneath bracken
that made rusty diamond flickers
of its own – all of which brought

a new kind of rush, a quickening
of my scamper down the slope
to the beach and the need
to find my father, waiting patiently
for the tale of my big adventure.

Doubtful Sound

Not a harbour or even a sound
after all, but a body of water
carved by a glacier, so deep
and black it's midnight
made of water. The captain steers

between the sheer granite cliffs –
land where no human has set foot –
cutting the engine, smalltalk, phones ...
and so we stand to command,
listening to the doubtful sound

of our own absence, black water
lapping against the hull somehow
inaudible, enhancing the quiet.
Everyone is so deep in their thoughts,
in silence, the whole idea of words

recedes like the tide, saltwater
hushed by fresh cascades
full of mountainous dark
reflecting the stars – a living map
of the past or some other half-

gleaned, mystical world, a lock-in
where the clock slips past twelve
unheard, and all the old codgers
have no need for conversation.
Fiordland penguins huddle at the bar

and a bottlenose dolphin muscles
a shining corkscrew from thin air.
A whiskered seal, lounging
in a big leather chair by the fire,
claps with one flipper.

Opal

Melvin, a location scout, guides me
between the pyramids of grit
towards the burrows, all the people
turned rabbit, or mole.

He shows me the fist-width holes
drilled into his kitchen wall
to store wine, later the massive borings
that make an underground church.

Then we're picking our way
through the fossickings and man-trap
mine shafts: stumble here in the dark
and it's a matter of seconds until

you feel your spine compacting
to dust. Melvin leads me in
by a safer, steadier descent
through the labyrinth – glowing red

with shafts of man-trap light
that now let us breathe – while he
turns trickster, a pair of copper rods
bent into his grip and randomly

swivelling. It has to be a con – yes? –
but as I take the rods in my own hands
I sense the circuitry, the subtle tug
of a living compass formed

by my trembling grasp as I'm drawn
to the thick, silicate streak in the rock,
a milky rainbowed cloud, enough
to make the live wires swing suddenly

apart in a sort of ecstasy. I stare
at the irrefutable gleam, jism
splashed through mother earth,
diffracting the light into pure bliss.

Potch the lot of it, surely, but Melvin
– with what licence I don't know –
breaks a piece from the crumbling wall
and presents it. To me. A gift. For you.

Instamatic

footprints in the sand
of a penguin's flight
from sea to the bush

✻

the drying splash
of a whale on lenses
peeled from my eyes

✻

somewhere in the mud
the mudbug – architect
of these dreaming mud spires

✻

a red melon mush
where the wallaby's head
was lopped by a quoll

✻

a roadside boulder that
moved ... square droppings ...
wombat ... not mad

✻

for the eagle-eyed
a pile of sticks
in a nested tree

✻

hello possum!
that hullaballoo on the roof
has to be you

✳

at dawn and dusk
binocular ripples
of the playful platypus

✳

tractor tyre tracks
of a loggerhead leaving
buried treasure on the beach

✳

the pink tentacle
of a jellyfish sting
across a woman's breast

✳

green-blue lightning
of a frog escaping
the kookaburra's beak

✳

cancerous scavengings
in the devil's jaw – last
refuge of the scoundrel

✳

in the rearview mirror
a snaking black crack
across the snaking road

Location Services

A four-metre bull male saltwater crocodile named Nigel
has been caught and electronically tagged, a tracking device
embedded in his neck, kept in place with a wadge of putty.
It's not just the kookaburras that are laughing, but Nigel
is sufficiently thick-skinned to think it's not at him.

For twelve months he cruises the South Alligator River
and beyond. The rangers map his movements, picking up
a GPS signal that shows him as a green line snaking
across a monitor screen. What they don't know, what nobody
would have guessed and what Nigel is totally oblivious to

is the river-level eye-balling that's rife, spreading rumour
of his whereabouts – except it's not rumour, it's gossip
fuelled by a facebook precision. That lump of putty
will be Nigel's undoing; for all his roving, everyone
suddenly has the measure of Nigel, has him pinned down.

At the year's end when Nigel, venturing back to his old haunts,
is once more roped around the jaw, hauled onto shore
and disconnected, the atmosphere on this stretch of water
has changed: younger males are truculent, females
strangely aloof; it seems that Nigel has become both legend

and outcast, achieved *annus mirabilis* and *horribilis* in one.
The rangers, meanwhile, take stock of their copious data,
making plans for Nigel that will keep him from the tourists,
knowing what's best for him – and them – but unaware
that the data is out of date, that nothing here is as it was.

Tinnitus

The cicadas have turned the volume
to 11. Is this a joke?
Their tiny red power-on lights
and plastic-y black grilles
are everywhere, studding
the pale eucalypt trunks,
pumping out a surround-
sound love song, five years
in the making.
                    Some
litter the ground, burnt out.

All conversation is eclipsed.
Whatever she is trying to tell him
fades to the silent movements
of her lips,
                    sweet nothings
like twists of paperbark
falling to the forest floor
today, tomorrow, this year
or next ...
                    The noise
is the hissing curse
of thinking *yes yes yes*
to every whispered offer
of *more*.
            And now
there's an underscore,
the thrumming bush telegraph
that mocks all regrets, the drum beat
of *what's done is done*

and no, this won't go away.

Bowerbird

All morning it was elusive. Then the weather
closed in with a vengeance, the dark sky

shredding itself and forcing a fire-lit refuge
with whisky to steady the nerves,

as if one paradise could be swopped
for another, happiness so tenacious.

Framed in the window, the drag of rain
was black and white, transmission failing

when colour kicked in: a regent bowerbird
with golden crown and golden eye,

feathers at full stretch, holding to the rain-
drenched bush being wrenched from its roots,

holding like the stubborn glow inside your skin
when you've glanced too close at the sun.

Terra Incognita

It starts as a game, clocking
features of the forest:
a dead stump with its tail
of strangler fig – a tyrannosaur;
a massive stinging tree
with hearts on its sleeve.

Then the track becomes less worn.
The track runs out.

Start again, with memory
your lifeline – keep talking
to yourself. Give things names.
It's the land of the parrots,
land of the parrots. Retrace
your steps – keep talking
to yourself. Give things names.

The spiral of black branches
above that pile of rocks
I'll call Snake Top, except now
it's snaked right out of sight,
and that startling pink leaf
has become one of many,
      blowing in the wind.
The mossed log with open jaws
is suddenly everywhere,
eating every crumb ...

It's dark. I'm stumbling.
I wanted to be back
from Gondwana in time for tea,
instead it's dark, I'm stumbling,
and each wrong turn
leaves a fresh, false trail ...

Wood for the Trees

The forest closes ranks,
protecting its last secrets.

What's left are stories,
a few photos

and digitized clips
of a tiger behind bars,

showing a marsupial pose
and bewilderment

that it should come to this:
stripes, skinned

from starkening ribs,
stretched and pinned

to a wall inscribed
with a roll call of killers.

One remaining foetus
floats in formaldehyde,

eyelids closed, oblivious
both to its demise

and the new bounty
on its head. I marvel

at the delicate solidity
of the unborn, half-

expecting the eyelid
to open and acknowledge

my disbelief that all this
is made of *wood* –

the animal alive
in the fluid grain – but

I can hear a gentle chisel
still at work, scrolling

furls of huon pine
to the thickening floor.

Cull

the nocturnal bristling
through pale green frost /

the compromised, the cornered
and provoked, the lost /

the inquisitive whiskers
still wanting some debate /

those keeping a roadside vigil
beside their lifeless mate /

crossbreeds minding their own business
beyond the barbed wire of the estate /

those too great, too white,
with too much cartilaginous might /

all the misplaced prodigies
suffering a homesick night /

the indigenous poor with too little
or too much sense of their plight /

the slivers of shadow
striped with moonlight /

anything with stripes on its face
or stripes in its name /

those harbouring disease
or anything on which to stick the blame /

those with better teeth
and many more of the same /

the colour-blind
lacking the need to blink /

those too much inclined
simply to think /

all the exceptions to the rules
the damned fools /

Fire

A shock of flame breaks
from the cathedral roof. Lead
melts and pieces of coloured glass
fall ...

Who knew there was a hidden forest
amongst all this stone?
                Black smoke
storms from the south transept
into the nave. The uproar
is like a waterfall
fighting with a waterfall,
water losing out to liquid lead.

The first of the firemen drops his head.

Oh for the wings, for the wings of a dove ...

A ribbon of smoke   wraps around the globe

           to where the sky now's also wrong, a dirty orange,
                   the Blue Mountains ablaze,
                     a break of flame cutting
               through the eucalyptus haze, smoke
                    drifting from the wilderness
                         to the city ...

                    We flick between the tv
         and the thick smoke drifting
across our own yards.

Fire flicks between the tinder-dry timber vaults
               and the forest; smoke blooming

from charred stone columns
 to fluted bark, the flammable skin
 shed by self-preserving trees,

 inferno
to inferno.

 And now it's about fighting fire
 with fire, blocking its rampage
 from one transept of the mountains
into the length of the nave.

 A global audience tunes in.
 It wants the story
 – any story will do
 if told by the flames.

Oh for the wings ... forty winks ...
a chorister's mischief,
like a dropped match
setting off this uproar in the aisles.

 The firemen are past exhaustion,
 one slumped beside his truck
 in a fluorescent surplice
 badged with latin:
 Orta Recens Quam Pura Nites.

 Just forty winks ...
 but he could sleep for the years it takes

for silence finally to descend.

 The wilderness
 is commandeered, hundreds of trees
heading for the cathedral yard.

Newly Risen How Brightly You Shine.
I walk through the restorations,
noting a splash of lead, a streak of soot,
a strip of blackened bark
on the stone floor beneath the rose window.

O for the wings, for the wings of a dove!
Far away, far away would I rove!

> *In the wilderness build me a nest,*
> *and remain there for ever at rest.*

A white bird lifts from the vault of trees,

> lifts from the vast cathedral roof.

Ode to Joy

The staggering journey is almost done,
the blood-orange sun sinking on cue
into the Southern Ocean,
the sense of closure so strong
that some of the cliff-top audience
are beginning to make tracks,
one whole crowd of Japanese tourists
already on the bus
when flying through the sea
comes a burst of homing energy
that self-prompts
its own standing ovation – too soon! –
with a plashing in the shallows,
so much formal attire all fittingly
drenched in champagne
while up in the gods we gasp
at the audacity – the crescendo
as each new jubilant wave of artists
joins the prolonged hurrah
of tingling feet, feet that make you think
at first they're through, finished,
but the tingling gets the better of them
and after each surge, each seemingly
satisfying crash onto the sand
and another tempting sight
of what must surely be the end,
there's a pull,

        an irresistible drag
once more into the orchestral surf
so that first one penguin
and then another,
with only just enough strength

to waddle up the beach,
turns for a further rush into the sea,
at which the whole brotherhood
is drawn back into the triumphal fun,
to more of this revelling in return,
the not-quite-done-dom
where those furthest along have no choice
but to halt, be patient,

                  until they too
can't resist one more frolic in the sublime
before the so-called comfort of a burrow
where they'll be out of their element
like music in silence, if silence
is ever reached –
it's becoming hard to believe
as yet another mischievous bed-timer
leads a rebellion into the watery fray
before, finally, calling it a day,
though day really is too small a word
for what will quiver through their bodies
as they dream a rapturous reprise.

The Submerged Cathedral

Others are more prepared,
with snorkels, flippers ...
I simply gulp the air and plunge
to see what treasures lie beneath –
my eyes adjusting to the mix
of camouflage and party gaiety,
energy and poise: gold
in the moving, mottled rock;
a sheet of sandpaper half-

hidden in the sand, betrayed
by its blink; a shoal like a choir
conducted by the sea. Names
elude me. I need to look,
remember, make a compendium
of fish in my head: fish
with thick, inquisitive lips;
fish opening their mouths
like communicants. Sunlight

filters down through the drift
of grainy bubbles as I glide
into a silent realm of stained glass.
I hang motionless while three
sleek silvery-mauve shapes
begin to circle me, before
vanishing as secretively
as they came. I take a final gulp,
stretching my lungs, holding it

as if forever – needing to hold
and decipher the calm for when
the familiar, land-lubbering threats,
perils and dangers of this night,
come crowding in once more
from all sides – as if oxygen
like knowledge, prayer, love,
was something to be sustained,
not endlessly replenished.

The Strong Country

The distance seemed interminable, but time
went more quickly if you split
from yourself and with hair in the wind
let the delicate beat of your horse's hooves

keep pace with the sweltering family saloon,
companionable but free, following the dead
straight empty outback trail in search
of recreation. Please? Please can I play?

*

The Romsey road would never be the A39.
For my father, a route required a destination,
not a number. In this, as in everything,
I would have backed him to the end.

What then to make of the Salisbury turning
deep in Dungog Shire? No one in this neck
of the woods with their ancient gums
has even heard of Strong & Co the brewery.

I'm suddenly at a loss. The radio has me
dashing through the snow – at 39 degrees
by the Micra's liquid crystal display.
Full-on, the air conditioning means nothing.

A weatherboard church stands in
for the cathedral, *letting me down,* while a fly
won't leave me alone. My mobile
shrugs: *No service. Low battery power.*

*

The absence seems interminable – our fathers
in their old Fords, eyes fixed on the road ahead
so that all we see is their clean shaven necks,
a trailer with everything we could possibly need

trundling behind. You're still riding alongside
when a sign – *You're in the Strong Country* –
looms from the New Forest dusk.
You grip the reins. I hold my nerve. Or try.

[73]